Field

Tony Ward

Printed in the United States of America
Designed by VAP Group Ltd
Cover design by William Seabright & Associates

00 99 98 97 96
10 9 8 7 6 5 4 3 2 1

Library of Congress Cataloging-in-Publication Data

Ward, Tony, 1931–
       Field / Tony Ward.
              p. cm. — (Olympic library)
       Includes index.
       Summary: Refers to famous performances while presenting an overview of the Olympic field
       events and providing information on how athletes train, qualify for, and participate in the
       games.
             ISBN 1-57572-038-8
             1. Track-athletics—Juvenile literature. 2. Jumping—Juvenile literature. 3. Weight
       throwing—Juvenile literature. [1. Track and field. 2. Jumping. 3. Olympics.] I. Title. II. Series.
       GV1060.5.W255 1996
       796.42—dc20   95-39284

Acknowledgments
The Publishers would like to thank the following for permission to reproduce photographs.
Cover photograph: Todd Warshaw/ALLSPORT Photography (USA) Inc.; ALLSPORT: p.9, 10, 20, 21, 22, 29; ALLSPORT
Historical Collection: p.27; Associated Sports Photography: p.12, 16; Colorsport: p.7, 8, 11, 13, 14, 15, 23, 24, 25, 26, 28; Dave
Black: p.17; Hirmer Fotoarchive: p.4; Popperfoto: p.5; Supersport Photographs/Eileen Langsley: p.6, 18, 19.

The Olympic rings logo is reproduced with the permission of the International Olympic Committee.

The Publisher gratefully acknowledges Mr. Robert Paul, consultant to the U.S. Olympic Committee, and Mr. Paul
Rowbotham for their comments on the manuscript.

Every effort has been made to contact copyright holders of any material reproduced in this book. Any omissions will be
rectified in subsequent printings if notice is given to the publisher.

Contents

Early years

The ancient Greeks believed in the idea of "a healthy mind in a healthy body." One of the ways they put this idea into practice was by holding running races and other sporting events in honor of Zeus, king of the gods. The ancient Olympic Games, which began in 776 B.C., originally lasted for one day but were eventually expanded to seven days.

When the ancient Games first began, there was just one contest, the **stadium race**. Other events were later added, including jumping and throwing. One of the most famous ancient Greek statues shows the athlete Discobolus in a position that all modern discus throwers would easily recognize. The long jump, which is still popular, was also an event at the ancient Games.

This statue of Discobolus shows the Greek ideal of physical perfection.

Did you know?

American Ray Ewry was the master of the three standing jumps, which were discontinued in 1912. He won the standing high jump gold in four Olympics, including the unofficial Games of 1906, his best distance being 5 feet, 2 inches at the London Games in 1908. Ewry also won gold four times in the standing long jump and twice in the standing triple jump.

The Modern Olympics

When the Frenchman Baron Pierre de Coubertin started the modern Olympic Games in Athens in 1896, three jumping events were included, as well as the shot put and the discus. American James Connolly became the first gold medal winner in a field event when he triumphed in the triple jump. So, since the earliest days of the modern Games, the field events have been a major part of the Olympics. Today, they comprise 8 of the 23 Olympic events.

In the early Games of the modern era, there were some field events that are no longer included and some rules that are no longer followed. There were three standing jumps—the high jump, the long jump, and the triple jump. The shot put and the discus were thrown with both hands, and the javelin was thrown any which way. There was also an event for throwing a 56-pound hammer.

Olympic Field Events

Men	Women
High jump	High jump
Long jump	Long jump
Triple jump	Triple jump
Shot put	Shot put
Discus throw	Discus throw
Javelin throw	Javelin throw
Pole vault	
Hammer throw	

The Hammering Irish

For hundreds of years, at local fairs and other festivals in Ireland, there was a contest for throwing the shafted hammer. So it is no surprise that Irish-born athletes won six of the first seven Olympic titles in the hammer throw. John Flanagan, an Irish American, won the first three golds. Pat O'Callaghan won the gold for Ireland in 1928 and 1932.

Women and Field Events

Women athletes entered the Olympics for the first time in 1928 at the Amsterdam Games, after a campaign by sportswomen around the world. In the next two Olympics, the only field events for women were the high jump and the discus. From 1936, women also competed in javelin throwing. Today, only the pole vault and the hammer events do not have women competitors. For the Olympic Games of 2000, it is expected that women will compete in all the field events.

John Flanagan, an Irish American, won the hammer throw at the 1904 Olympic Games.

Getting Nervous

Not many people in the world have the talent and good luck to become a member of their country's Olympic team. For those who do, it is an experience they will remember for the rest of their lives.

As the Olympic Games approach, those field event athletes who have been on their country's team before hope that they will have that honor again. Other athletes hope that they will become members of the elite club of Olympians.

Injury Can Mean Disaster

Some athletes miss the Olympics because of injury or poor performance. British javelin thrower Tessa Sanderson, for example, attended her first Olympics at Montreal in 1976, her second at Moscow in 1980, and her third at Los Angeles in 1984 where she won gold in the javelin. Unfortunately, she was badly injured in 1988 just before the Games at Seoul began. She recovered, however, and qualified for Barcelona in 1992. Sanderson is the only British female field event athlete to have been selected for five different Games.

Fear of injury grows as the Games get closer. In the United States, a competitor has to qualify by being in the top three in the national Olympic trials. No excuses are accepted. If an athlete does not compete in the trials because of an injury, even if that injury is expected to clear up by the time the Games take place, then that athlete loses any chance of being selected—even if he or she is the world record holder! In Great Britain, up to two competitors in any event can be selected even if they did not win or place in the national trials.

A young athlete is coached for a throwing event.

In the time leading up to the Barcelona Olympics in 1992, top athletes around the world were being selected for their national teams. American Jackie Joyner-Kersee, like Tessa Sanderson, overcame an injury to qualify for the long jump and the **heptathlon**. In the Ukraine, the world's greatest pole vaulter, Sergey Bubka, was chosen to defend his title. Carl Lewis and Mike Powell, American rivals in the long jump, both qualified by coming in first and second in the trials. Only a year earlier at the Tokyo World Championships in 1991, both had broken one of the oldest records in field athletics. For 23 years, American Bob Beamon had held the long jump record with 29 feet, $2^{1}/_{2}$ inches in the 1968 Mexico City Olympics. In 1991, Powell and Lewis both exceeded Beamon's distance, with Powell winning with 29 feet, $4^{1}/_{2}$ inches.

Steve Backley, a British javelin thrower, won a bronze medal at the 1992 Barcelona Olympics.

Did you know?

The favorite to win the women's javelin event at the 1964 Olympics in Tokyo was Soviet Elvira Ozilina. When she only finished fifth, she was so disappointed that she shaved her head!

Off to the Games!

For many athletes, just making the Olympic team fulfills their dreams. When they go to the Games, they will do their best, but everyone knows that only three competitors in each event will take medals home. For them, the main goal is to qualify for the final of their field event.

The Buildup

After the great feeling of being selected has worn off, all the field athletes know that they have to work hard to keep in shape, avoid injury, and try to build to their **peak** for the Games. If an athlete hasn't managed to get the combination of training and competing just right, he or she can hit peak **form** either before or after the Games.

U.S. decathlete David Johnson excels at the shot put.

Did you know?

At the Paris Games in 1900, many of the best discus throws became entangled in the branches of the trees that lined the throwing area and so could not be measured!

In the meantime, the competitions carry on. In the period just before the Olympics there are many world-class **meets** in Europe. Before the Barcelona Games, all the best American athletes attended and competed in them as well. These various meets make a tough schedule for the athletes, but because many of them receive **appearance money**, it is part of their "job" as full-time athletes to compete.

In the weeks leading up to the Games, Olympic uniforms are provided for the national teams by their National Olympic Committee. The uniform can include special suits, track suits, and shoes. For some field sports the competitors have to have special equipment, such as the belts worn by the shot putters and the javelin throwers, made for their event.

Team members usually travel together, sometimes attending training camps near the Olympic city for last-minute improvements and the opportunity to adjust to a different climate or time zone. Whether they arrive direct from their home country or from training camp, as the Games draw nearer all the athletes know that it is now "make or break" time.

Mike Powell trains for the long jump in preparation for the 1992 Olympic Games.

In the Olympic City

Athletes from around the world converge on the Olympic city. The airport is full of tall high jumpers, strong pole vaulters, and huge throwers being greeted by receptionists and Olympic clerks wearing colorful uniforms. They are ushered through the airport and taken by buses to the Olympic Village, which will be their home for the duration of the Games.

In the Village

At the Barcelona Games in 1992, the Village was one of the best ever built. It nestled on the shores of the Mediterranean Sea like a town within a town.

National teams stay together in the same section of the Village. Within that national area, the various sports

Jump training includes the use of weights in order to push the athletes harder.

In the Olympic Village, many athletes exchange their country's badges at the "pin marketplace."

and events are grouped together. The "heavies," like the throwers, are housed together, practice together, and eat together (usually large quantities!). Many of the athletes from the different countries already know each other.

All the athletes eat in the big self-service restaurant in the Village. Every athlete knows what diet to follow, and every diet is catered to. The distance runners eat as many **carbohydrates** as possible, and the big throwers eat a diet with as much bulk as possible. Many of the athletes also take vitamin supplements to help them recover from all their hard training and pre-Olympic competition.

The security at the Village and the site of the Games is tight but not overwhelming. All bags and equipment are electronically checked every time an athlete enters the Village or the Olympic Stadium.

The Opening Ceremony

Most of the athletes take part in the magnificent opening ceremony, where all the national teams march around the Stadium to the applause of the huge crowd. Because the field events take place in the second half of the Games, the competitors still have time to train and relax before it all begins for them.

Once the opening ceremony is over, everyone is anxious for the Games to begin. During the tense waiting period, the team **physical therapist** works overtime as the competitors worry over the slightest ache or pain. As the time for the field events approaches, each team holds meetings where managers and coaches give out all the information the athletes require, including their competitors' numbers. At this time, the throwers and jumpers have to focus on themselves and their events. This is the moment when, for them, the Games really begin.

In Action

In the buses, as they are being taken to the Olympic stadium for the qualifying round of their competition, most athletes sit in silence. They don't speak to each other or to the coaches and managers who go with them on the journey. Athletes are in what the great American 400-meter runner Lee Evans once called a "pre-event trance." They don't want their minds taken off the jobs they have to do.

The Qualifying Round

In field events, the object of the qualifying round is for athletes to achieve the distance or height set by the organizers that will automatically let them pass on into the final round. Each competitor has three attempts. No athlete feels safe at this time because the history of athletics is filled with great champions who failed to qualify for the finals, even when they were the favorite to win. In 1960 in Rome, for example, Mary Rand of Great Britain, a great favorite in the long jump, did not make it to the final round. In 1991, Steve Backley of Great Britain, then the European javelin champion, failed to qualify for the final round at the World Championship in Tokyo. Nobody wants to become another story of lost chances.

Carl Lewis focuses on the opening round of the long jump event at the 1992 Games.

The coach drops off the competitors at the warm-up track. Each country has its own team headquarters here, usually surrounding the physical therapists' training tables that are set up in any available shade. The athletes work on their **warm-ups** slowly, timing them to finish just before they are called to go with the clerks to the Olympic Stadium for their event. Everyone walks to the reception area at the Stadium, champions and first-timers sitting together as they wait.

Mistakes Mean Disaster

The competitors are divided into two groups or "pools" for the qualifying round. A mistake at this time can be a disaster. Misjudging a run-up can mean not making it to the finals. Some jumpers and throwers have traveled thousands of miles and ended their Olympic careers with three no-jumps or three no-throws in the qualifying round. No matter how well athletes do in the qualifying round, they have it all to do over again. In the final the next day, all those who made it through start from the beginning again.

Once the qualifying round is over, the competitors can leave the Stadium. Some go back to the warm-up track for final preparations. Others quickly return to the buses, their dreams dashed.

For the successful, the first part of the task is over, but gold, silver, and bronze will be decided on the following day.

Steve Backley qualifies in the javelin event in the 1992 Games.

13

Behind the Scenes

Major sporting events such as the Olympic Games could not take place without the assistance and dedication of thousands of volunteer helpers.

Judges and Officials

Some sports such as football and hockey only need a small number of officials. In field events, almost a whole army of officials is needed, even though electronic measuring devices are in use at all international competitions. Unfortunately, there is no electronic device that can rake a jumping pit, replace high jump and pole vault bars, or collect thrown javelins, hammers, discuses, and shots!

In the long and triple jumps, competitors must complete **take-off** on or behind a board on the ground, and a key judge decides the **validity** of any leap. A small area of claylike plasticine just in front of the board will show marks from the competitors' shoes, which will help the judge to make a decision. In the throwing events, athletes must stay within a circle or behind a line on a runway for the javelin throw to be valid. In the high jump and in the pole vault, athletes must not go beyond an imaginary line drawn between the two uprights before starting the jump. Judges are required to make decisions on all of these starts. Other judges are needed to place markers showing where throwing implements have landed. In the long throws, a special electronic eye high up in one of the stands can then measure the throw. In the shot put, the measuring is done by judges using a tape.

Each event has a chief judge. There is usually a jump referee and a throws referee in charge of their events, and their word is final. Any protests are dealt with by a Jury of Appeal appointed by the International Amateur Athletics Federation (**I.A.A.F.**), the world governing body for track and field.

Field event officials in action

Clerks and media join competitors on Carl Lewis's long jump victory lap at the 1992 Games.

Drug Testing

Specialist officials deal with **drug control**. Athletes are chosen at random and are informed after an event that they must have a test for drugs or **banned substances**. This test has to be taken within one hour of the athlete being informed. Any athlete who sets a national or world record is automatically tested.

The use of banned substances is a big menace in field competitions. The most dangerous drugs, and the ones that carry a **mandatory ban** as a punishment, are **anabolic steroids**. Many drugs can cause an athlete serious illnesses later in life, as well as the risks at the time they are taken. The German heptathlete Birgit Dressel died during the 1980s from a cocktail of drugs she took to improve her performance. Drug taking in sport is cheating. When athletes are caught, they bring disgrace not only on themselves, but also on their teammates, their families, and even their country.

National Team Officials

Most national teams have a team manager and a head coach. They work hard for the team while they are at the Olympics, trying to meet every individual need. There may also be specialist coaches for the different events. On the medical side, each team travels with doctors, physical therapists, and masseurs. This medical team is overworked as the athletes complete their final preparations and worry about their health and possible injuries. Without all these officials, most of whom work without pay, field sports would not be able to function.

Fulfilling the Dream

Carl Lewis won his third gold medal in 1992 in Barcelona.

It is the second to the last day of the 1992 Olympic Games, and the weather is hot and sunny. For Heike Drechsler it is a day that has been a long time coming. She has had to wait for more than a week as her German teammates compete and then celebrate winning their medals. She has even seen her great rival, Jackie Joyner-Kersee, win a gold medal in the heptathlon after only two days of competition. Now she hopes it is her turn.

Drechsler, a former East German (**G.D.R.**) athlete, won the first ever world title in 1983 when she was only 18 years old. She had missed the Los Angeles Games in 1984 because of the **boycott** by the Soviet Union and all Eastern European countries (except Romania) and came in second to Joyner-Kersee at the Seoul Games in 1988.

The competitors walk up to the long jump pit in single file to where the officials await them. Then they warm up, practice their **run-ups**, and generally get ready for their big moment.

This Is It!

In the first round it is clear that the competition is between Inessa Kravets of Ukraine, Drechsler, and Joyner-Kersee. At the end of the first round, it is Kravets first, Joyner-Kersee second, and Drechsler third.

U.S. decathlete Dan O'Brien is a masterful pole-vaulter.

Drechsler improves her distance as the final continues, while Kravets and Joyner-Kersee can't improve on their first-round distances. In the fourth round, Drechsler jumps the 23 feet, $5\frac{1}{4}$ inches that gives her the gold medal. The crowd roars its support at the medals ceremony, and she hears the German national anthem played for her victory.

Elsewhere in Barcelona that week, Carl Lewis became the first long jumper in history to win three consecutive gold medals. He beat teammate Mike Powell by only $1\frac{1}{4}$ inches. Sergey Bubka did not have a good Games. After failing to vault his chosen **opening height** after three attempts, his chances of a medal were gone.

Tessa Sanderson, at age 36, finished fourth in this, her last, Olympics. She proudly joined the other athletes in the memorable closing ceremony. But was this Sanderson's final Games? In 1995 she asked to be put on the British International Drug Register, something that she had to do if she were going to compete in 1996. Only one other woman athlete, Lia Manolou of Romania, has competed in six Olympic Games. Sanderson would also be the oldest woman ever to compete in the Olympic javelin event.

Did you know?

Al Joyner of the United States won the triple jump at the 1984 Games in Los Angeles. He is the brother of Jackie Joyner-Kersee. A year after his 1984 victory, he married Florence Griffiths ("Flo-Jo"), who won gold in both women's sprint races at the 1988 Olympics in Seoul.

Making the Commitment

Many young athletes dream of one day competing at the Olympics and maybe even winning the greatest of all sporting prizes: an Olympic gold medal. Those who want a chance at gold have to make a definite commitment to their sport, often from quite early in their lives.

School Days

Most careers in field events start when a boy or girl finds out that he or she can jump or throw much better than other children. This can lead young athletes to a chance to represent their school in competitions at higher and higher levels.

By this time the successful and talented young athlete has joined a track and field club and has a coach to help with training.

Every young field event athlete should make sure that his or her chosen club and coach have good reputations and properly qualified staffs. In the United States, much of the high-level training is not done in clubs but in schools and colleges. The coaches at U.S. colleges are professional.

In field events, it is vitally important for a young competitor to learn the correct methods right from the beginning. A skilled coach can make sure that a field event athlete does not develop a sloppy **technique**, which can be very hard to unlearn and sometimes even dangerous. A good coach also knows when throwers can move from one weight of implement to a heavier one as they get older and stronger.

A British high jumper competes for his school.

As field event athletes get older, they have chances to get involved in specialist training. For example, throwers spend a lot of time weight training, but it is important not to start this when an athlete is too young. Jumpers do a lot of bounding exercises, but when they start and how much they do must be monitored.

Many great American champions started in their state's high school championships. By the time a young field event athlete reaches college level, a commitment to the sport has been made. In Great Britain, long jumper Mary Rand, javelin thrower Fatima Whitbread, and double Olympic champion decathlete Daley Thompson all started their high-level careers at the National Schools Championships.

Sticking With One Coach

A number of famous field event athletes have had the same coach since they were very young. Carl Lewis has always been coached by Tom Tellez. And Steve Backley, since the age of 18, has always been coached by John Trower.

When young field event athletes finish school, a decision has to be made as to whether there is a future for them at a high level in the sport. Coaches and family have to help as young competitors look deep within themselves to see if there is the will to train hard and explore their talent to the maximum. They know it won't be easy.

A young international thrower practices with his coach.

CARL LEWIS CASE STUDY

Born: July 1, 1961, Birmingham, Alabama

Attended the University of Houston in Texas

Coached by Tom Tellez

Despite not being the world record holder, Carl Lewis is the greatest long jumper of all time. He has 12 of the top 20 jumps ever achieved and has won three Olympic golds and three world titles in this event.

From February 1981 until his great competition with fellow-American Mike Powell, at the World Championship in Tokyo in 1991, Carl won 65 long jumps in a row, coming out on top at every high level meet he entered.

As a true all-around athlete, Lewis has also won gold medals in two Olympic 100 meter races, one 200 meter race, and as a member of two Olympic sprint relay teams.

Making the Grade

Steve Smith set a world record at the 1992 World Junior Championships in Seoul.

For young field event athletes under the age of 20, there are many opportunities for international competition. In Europe there are junior championships every two years. In the Americas, there are the Pan-American Junior Championships every four years. And for all young athletes there are the World Junior Championships every two years.

By the time they reach this level of competition, athletes are training hard every day of the week. For field event athletes who live in colder climates, the chance to use indoor training facilities is vitally important during the winter months. Young field event athletes also need to have access to weight training.

Not many field event athletes can make enough money from appearances or through sponsorship to decide to become full-time athletes, as often happens at the highest level in track. Field event athletes have to train when they aren't at college or work, which makes it more difficult for them to make it to the top.

Success as a Junior

Being selected for a European, Pan-American, or World Junior championship means that the field event athlete can gain valuable international experience. The arrangements the young athlete experiences—the accommodations, the transportation, and the reporting procedures—are almost identical to those used at the Olympic Games. This means that young athletes can gradually get used to the stresses of major championships such as the Olympics.

Many world junior medalists go on to make it at the senior level. Javier Sotomayor of Cuba went on to become the world record holder for the high jump after having started as the World Junior champion in 1986. Ilke Wyludda (Germany) in the discus, Galina Astafei (then of Romania, now Germany) in the high jump, and Steve Smith (Great Britain) have all achieved medals at major world competitions after good careers as junior champions. In fact, Steve Smith, who was the World Junior high jump champion of 1992, jumped higher at the Juniors in Seoul in 1991 than the gold medal winner did a year later at the Barcelona Olympics!

Being a success at junior level does not mean automatic success at senior level. The years just after the end of junior competition are vital for the young field event athlete who will need help, support, and encouragement.

All athletes, at this critical point, dream of future success at European, Pan-American, World, and then, most important, Olympic level.

Viktor Chistyakov won the pole vault at the 1994 World Junior Championships in Lisbon.

Did you know?

Fanny Blankers-Koen, a great Dutch athlete, was prevented from winning a fifth gold at the London Games in 1948 by a rule that then said women could only compete in three individual events. She had added the relay gold to individual golds for the 100-meter hurdles and the 200- and 100-meter sprinting events.

Getting to the Top

In field athletics, there is a full calendar of events at international level every single year. The days are long gone when a top athlete could have a year free of commitment to major championships.

Field event athletes keep up a full schedule of training, including special diets, to be sure that their techniques are reaching perfect form as the time for international competitions approaches.

The "heavy" throwers need to eat large quantities of food because they use up huge quantities of energy with their power training. Not many field event athletes can devote all their time and energy to training because only a few—such as Carl Lewis, Steve Smith, Steve Backley, and Dalton Grant—really consider themselves to be full-time athletes. Jobs and education have to come first for all the others.

Selection for International Events

Being selected to represent their country at international athletic events is a stepping stone for some field event athletes on their path to the Olympic Games. In some field events, all of the main international competitors come from one part of the world, so an international event in one area can be almost like a mini-Olympics. For many years, for example, the former Soviet Union was so powerful in the hammer throw event that being chosen to represent the U.S.S.R. was almost a guarantee of a medal at the Olympics!

Competition at high level in field events is tough, and winning the World Championship one year does not necessarily mean success at the Olympics the next year.

Sergey Bubka of the Ukraine wins the pole vault at the 1993 World Championships in Stuttgart.

Of all the field event world champions at Tokyo in 1991, only one, the German high jumper Heike Henkel, was successful in Barcelona in 1992.

An athlete to look for in future Games is Jonathon Edwards, a British triple jumper, who came to sudden prominence in the 1995 World Championships, where he broke the world record twice to become World Champion. He threatened the record in nearly every competition and has been described in the media as "Beamonesque."

If an athlete is selected to compete in a field event at the World Championships the year before the Olympic Games and manages to stay fit and injury-free, chances are good that he or she will make it through to national selection again.

World Championship selection identifies an athlete as a major contender, even if not a gold medalist. For example, Fatima Whitbread of Great Britain, who was the winner of the World Championship in the javelin in 1987 went on to win the silver medal at Seoul in 1988. Carl Lewis won three world championships and then the gold medals in the long jump in the Olympic Games that followed each of those wins. Great Britain's javelin thrower Steve Backley won European and Commonwealth Games titles in the lead-up to his bronze medal win at the Barcelona Olympics in 1992.

All international victories are hard to win, and the field event athletes who come in on top at high-level competitions enjoy their successes, but it is the gold at the Olympic Games every four years that is the ultimate prize.

Looking Back

Mary Peters, the British pentathlon gold medalist, smiles at Munich in 1972.

One of the greatest field event feats ever came in 1968 at the Mexico City Games. In his very first jump of the competition, Bob Beamon set a world record of 29 feet, $2\frac{1}{2}$ inches in the long jump, 22 inches further than the previous mark. This record stood for 23 years, until it was finally beaten by Mike Powell at the World Championships in Tokyo in 1991.

The decathlon has produced some great champions. The American Bob Mathias was the youngest ever Olympic men's champion. He was 17 years, 263 days old when he won gold at the London Games in 1948. He won again in 1952. The other double Olympic champion in this event was Great Britain's Daley Thompson. He won gold in 1980 and 1984, setting a world record in Los Angeles.

In 1968, the high jump in Mexico City was won by American Dick Fosbury, who used a new style of jump. He made the clearance by launching himself over head first with his back arched over the bar. This amazing innovation became known as the Fosbury Flop and is now used by many athletes.

Scandinavian countries won 10 out of the 17 javelin titles since this event was introduced in 1912. Of the 10, Finnish throwers won 6. It is not surprising to learn that javelin throwing is considered the national sport of Finland.

Daley Thompson, British decathlon champion, was in the 110-meter hurdles at the 1984 Los Angeles Olympics.

Great Britain's unluckiest woman medalist was Dorothy Odam-Taylor. In both 1936 in Berlin and 1948 in London, she finished second, even though she cleared the same height as the winner. In both cases she would have won under the rules as they now stand. Sixteen years after her first Olympic performance she competed in the 1952 Games in Helsinki and tied seventh. She also took part in the 1956 Games in Melbourne.

The five-event pentathlon was introduced to the Olympics in 1964. In 1972 at the Munich Games, Great Britain's Mary Peters beat the German favorite Heidi Rosendahl and set a world record. In 1984, two extra events were added to the pentathlon, so the event became known as the heptathlon. The greatest all-around athlete to win this event to date is Jackie Joyner-Kersee of the United States at Seoul in 1988 and again at Barcelona in 1992.

Olympic Heroes and Heroines

Al Oerter is a four-time winner of the Olympic discus event.

Some athletes dominate their event so much that they become legends. One such legend is the American discus thrower Al Oerter. During a period of 12 years from 1956 to 1968, he won 4 Olympic golds. This has never happened before or since. At each of his victories he set an Olympic record. In 1977, he came out of athletic retirement to train for the 1980 Olympics, and he came in fourth at the U.S. trials at the age of 44!

Another great field athlete is Viktor Sanyev of the Soviet Union. He won three titles and nearly captured a fourth when he finished second at the Moscow Games in 1980.

The Native American decathlon champion of 1912, Jim Thorpe, was **disqualified** four months after his victory when it was discovered that he had played minor league baseball for money—making him a professional, not an amateur sportsman. In 1983, years after Thorpe's death, the International Olympic Committee reinstated him as the joint medalist along with Hugo Wielander of Sweden, who had been awarded Thorpe's gold for the decathlon and pentathlon.

Did you know?

Imre Nemeth of Hungary won the discus at the London Games in 1948. His son Miklos won a gold medal in the javelin 28 years later at the Montreal Games.

Dick Fosbury won the high jump at the 1968 Mexico Olympics, using the revolutionary technique that now bears his name.

The greatest ever female Olympic field event gold medalist was the Russian thrower Tamara Press. Winner of the shot put event at Rome in 1960, she also won both the shot put and discus golds in Tokyo four years later with Olympic record-breaking throws. Sporting excellence was a family quality since Tamara's sister, Irina, won the first pentathlon in Tokyo, beating Britain's Mary Rand.

The first ever women's javelin champion at the Olympic Games was the American Mildred "Babe" Didrikson. Many think she was the greatest all-around sportswoman ever. At the 1932 Games in Los Angeles, she also won the 80-meter hurdles and took the silver medal in the high jump. After her success in track and field, she took up golf and established women's professional golf in the United States.

Ulrike Meyfarth of Germany was the youngest ever high jump champion. She won in her home city of Munich at the Games in 1972 when she was 16 years, 123 days old. After some years away from the sport, she returned to the Olympics at Los Angeles in 1984 to win gold again, this time as the oldest ever high jump champion at 28 years of age!

In 1952 at Helsinki, American Parry O'Brien won the first of two Olympic shot put titles. He repeated this in 1956 in Melbourne. He revolutionized the event by starting his swing at the back of the circle with his back turned away from the putting area. This gave him room for an extra half turn to gain more **momentum**. He went on to win at 116 top-level competitions in a row, and he became the first man to put over 60 feet.

Fantastic Field

In 1900 at Paris, Jakob Kauser of Hungary competed in the pole vault at the age of 13 years, 196 days. The youngest ever female competitor in any field event was Cindy Gilbert of the United States, who competed at age 15 years, 97 days alongside Ulrike Meyfarth, who went on to win the gold in the high jump.

Still Competing

The oldest men's gold medalist was Patrick Ryan of the United States, who won the hammer throw at Antwerp in 1920, when he was 37 years, 226 days old. The oldest man to compete in a field event was Trantisek Janda-Suk of Czechoslovakia who was 46 years, 111 days old when he competed at Paris in 1924.

The oldest woman to win a field event gold medal was Lia Manoliu from Romania. She won the discus gold in 1968 at Mexico City at the age of 36 years, 176 days. Four years later, at the age of 40, she became the oldest woman competitor in a field event.

Olympic Marriages and Romance

There have been some Olympic husband and wife partnerships. In 1952, Dana Zatopekova won the javelin on the same day that her husband, Emil Zatopek, took the gold in the 5,000 meters, one of his three golds that year. In 1968 at Mexico City, Sheila Sherwood won the silver in the long jump, and her husband,

American Jackie Joyner-Kersee, performed the heptathlon high jump at the Barcelona Olympics, 1992.

John Sherwood, won the bronze medal in the 400-meter hurdles.

At the Melbourne Games in 1956, American Harold Connolly won the hammer throw and also met his future wife, the discus champion from Czechoslovakia, Olga Fikotova. Despite huge administrative problems put in their way by both their governments, they were married in 1957 with Emil Zatopek acting as best man.

Breaking Six Feet

At Tokyo in 1964, Iolanda Balas of Romania won her second Olympic gold medal in the high jump. She was one of the greatest ever at this event and was never beaten in 140 consecutive high-level meets between 1956 and 1966. She was the first woman to jump more than six feet.

Did you know?

In 1924, DeHart Hubbard became the first African American man to win an individual gold medal when he triumphed in the long jump. In 1948, high jumper Alice Coachman became the first African American woman to win an Olympic title.

Sergey Bubka of the Ukraine celebrates a vault at the 1991 Moscow Grand Prix.

Glossary

anabolic steroids powerful performance-enhancing drugs

appearance money compensation paid to an athlete to compete at a meeting

banned substances illegal drugs that can give people who use them better performances, but using them can injure the user's health and is considered cheating

boycott deciding not to compete at an Olympic Games, usually for political reasons

carbohydrates compound nutrients found in such foods as potatoes and pasta

decathlon Olympic event with 10 disciplines

discus throw event in which a wooden or plastic disk is thrown for distance

disqualified banned from an event for breaking the rules of a competition or of a sport

drug control the testing of athletes for the use of banned substances after each event; room at the Stadium used for that testing

drugs register list of names from which athletes are chosen for Out-of-Competition Testing

form current standard

G.D.R. German Democratic Republic (formerly East Germany)

hammer throw Olympic event in which a metal sphere called a hammer is thrown for distance

heptathlon Olympic event having 7 disciplines

high jump an Olympic jumping event

I.A.A.F. International Amateur Athletics Federation, which governs world track and field

javelin throw Olympic event in which a thin metal shaft is thrown for distance

jumps referee person in charge of all judging of jumping events

long jumps an Olympic jumping event

mandatory ban prohibition, usually for drug taking, that must be imposed

meet a competition in which athletes match skills

momentum moving force or energy needed by athletes to perform at their best

national trials a country's meet to select an Olympic team

U.S.O.C. United States Olympic Committee, which represents all Olympic sports in the country

Olympic Village place that houses all the competitors and team management

opening height the height in the high jump or the pole vault events at which the competition begins

peak at one's best standard

physical therapist a person trained to prevent and treat sports injuries

pole vault an Olympic jumping event

run-up the run that jumping event athletes perform to gain momentum before they leap

scratch at, or as at, the start

shot put Olympic throwing event in which a metal sphere is heaved for distance

stadium race an event in the ancient Olympics

take-off the point at which an athlete leaps into the air in a jumping event

technique method used by athletes to perform their event

throws referee person in charge of all judging in throwing events

triple jump an Olympic jumping event

warm-up exercises performed before an event to make muscles ready to be used

validity official recognition of something being true

Index

Numbers in plain type (4) refer to the text. Numbers in italic type (*13*) refer to captions.